RUSTIC ELEGANCE ON NATURE'S EDGE.

The 46-room ocean-front Wickaninnish Inn is a natural destination resort on the extreme west coast of Vancouver Island in the renowned Clayoquot Sound region.

Perched on a rocky promontory at Chesterman Beach overlooking the open Pacific Ocean, it's also home to the Pointe Restaurant and On-the-Rocks Bar. Adding to the guest experience, the inn opened Ancient Cedars Spa in January 1999, North America's westernmost full-service spa facility. The inn's design plays rusticity against elegance throughout with the work of local artisans contributing to the ambiance. Each of its generously large guest rooms takes advantage of its surroundings with ocean view, private balcony, fireplace and soaker tub - all essential elements for a West Coast experience.

The multi-million project was the dream of long-time Tofino resident, Dr. Howard McDiarmid. It was inspired by the former historic Wickaninnish Inn of Long Beach, which was converted to a marine interpretive centre in the late 1970s after the creation of the Pacific Rim National Park. The new inn is located seven kilometres north of the park and with its name, spirit and style inspired from the former inn, the legacy of The Wickaninnish being a haven to world travellers continues.

The "reality" is an exclusive resort on "nature's edge", at the doorstep to world-class outdoor activities such as whale watching, storm watching, beachcombing, surfing and diving. Here, the weather plays a key role, enabling visitors to witness the romance of a crimson sunset to the fury and drama of a west coast winter storm. The latter is most evident from November to February, when 25 foot breakers are not uncommon. In spite of dramatic seas, this area is the warmest winter spot in Canada and glorious sunny days are also enjoyed during this season. The phenomenon of the gray whale migration makes for awesome entertainment from late February through May when 21,000 of these magnificent creatures pass by en route to the Bering Sea.

Since its opening in August of 1996, many accolades have been bestowed upon The Wickaninnish Inn. Of note is its designation as a member of the prestigious Relais & Châteaux group. It was also named a Top Hideaway for 1997 by Harper's Hideaways and made the 1999 Abercrombie and Kent Top 100 list. Also in 1999, Manager Charles McDiarmid won the Pinnacle Award as that year's Hotelier of the Year. And just this year the inn was rated "Best in the Country" by the renowned Zagat Guide. Reservations, rates and package information for both the inn and the restaurant can be obtained by calling toll-free in the USA and Canada to 1-800-333-4604, via any Relais & Châteaux international reservations office or via e-mail at wick@wickinn.com

RELAIS &
CHATEAUX

THE
Pointe
RESTAURANT

Ancient Cedars Spa
AT THE WICKANINNISH INN

www.wickinn.com

ISLAND EDENS

VICTORIA & LONG BEACH

RUSS HEINL

Photographs copyright© 2001 by
Russ Heinl

Text copyright© 2001 by
Rosemary Neering

Design by
Ken Seabrook Design

Photograph on page 39 by
Janet Dwyer

Published by
The Russ Heinl Group
Sidney, British Columbia
email: shotfromabove@mybc.com

Russ Heinl's images are available from:
Image Network Inc.
16 East 3rd Avenue
Vancouver, BC, Canada V5T 1C3
Ph: (604) 879-2533
Fx: (604) 879-1290
Email: twood@direct.ca

Printed in Canada.

ISBN O-9689219-0-6

previous page:
The sun sets over Vancouver Island.

CONTENTS

A CONTRAST OF EDENS

Back in 1860, thousands of miners made their way up to British Columbia's Cariboo country, where they worked through spring, summer and fall, plagued by mud and mosquitoes. But once winter threatened, they hastened down the trails and onto the boats that would take them somewhere more civilized: the infant town of Victoria on the southern tip of Vancouver Island. The mountains and mines served for the making of money, but when it came time for rest and relaxation, Victoria was the place to be.

They voted with their boots, underlining the verdict pronounced by fur trader James Douglas some twenty years earlier. Seeing for the first time the land where he would build his fur trading post, he was entranced by the meadows, covered by blue-flowering camas that spread under oak and arbutus north from the shore of Juan de Fuca Strait. He was equally impressed by the natural harbour, well-protected from the ocean storms. This gentle land, he wrote, was "a perfect Eden."

Douglas went on to become governor of both Vancouver Island and the mainland territory. Victoria went on to justify his words: the reputation of the region as a welcoming Eden has been sustained over the years. Gardens flourish, the climate is mellow, and the city has taken on the verdant aura of its surroundings.

It has grown greatly from those early and idyllic days. A metropolitan region that houses some 350,000 people, it greets four million tourists every year. Yet it retains that sense that Douglas and the miners so valued, of a pleasant gentle place. Its downtown centres on the area where Douglas's fort was originally built, where the buildings are determinedly low-rise and the streetscape on a human scale. Recent changes along the harbour and seafront mean that a stroller can walk some eleven kilometres on waterfront paths, around the harbour shore, through downtown, and along the open ocean, watching the seaplanes and the ships come and go.

Anywhere in this area, the visitor is never far from trees and flowers, those traditional components of Eden. Hanging baskets ornament every downtown street in summer; almost every house has its garden. Flowerbeds surround the Parliament Buildings and the nearby Empress Hotel. Flowering trees line city streets. Just outside downtown, the view that so entranced James Douglas still exists. In a remarkably prescient move, he decreed

opposite page: Boats in Victoria's Inner Harbour and the Empress Hotel, Victoria Conference Centre and Crystal Garden, seen from the sky.

above: *Downtown greeter Captain George at work.*

that the clifftop area north from the waterfront would be preserved for the enjoyment of all; those seventy-four hectares now form the semi-wild, semi-cultured Beacon Hill Park, with its serendipitous combination of rose gardens and ponds with Garry oaks, arbutus, Douglas fir, and imported exotic trees.

Though the city has spread well out from its downtown core, and suburbs surround Victoria, it's still not far to untouched seacoast and country landscapes. North of Victoria lies the Saanich Peninsula, where roads lead through undulating farmland and past the Butchart Gardens, probably the best-known attraction in western Canada. Upwards of a million visitors visit the gardens every year, to view the sunken, Japanese, Italian and rose gardens, and the display that changes with the seasons, from the earliest spring narcissi and brilliant tulips through the roses of summer, the colours of autumn, and the Christmas lights.

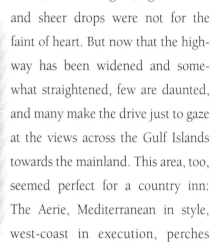

West from Victoria, narrow coastal roads meander through suburbs to rural landscapes where forest alternates with farms. In this area, the maturing of a Victoria tradition is visible. In the early days, settlers would ride out from the city to dine and stay at hostelries in the countryside. As more and more latter-day travellers sought the tranquillity of a rural setting and closeness to the sea, classic country inns and a plethora of bed and breakfasts opened to serve them out along the west-coast road. One of the earliest, and certainly the best-known, is the Sooke Harbour House, where many an acolyte comes to sample the famed west-coast cuisine and stay in the eclectic rooms.

To head up-island from Victoria, the driver must take the highway along the Malahat Ridge. For decades, "they" said it couldn't be done: building a road across the craggy Malahat that rose steeply from Finlayson Arm was simply too difficult, and an alternate route must be devised. Those who ventured across the Malahat after a crude road was first pushed through might have wished that alternate route had been discovered, for the heights, tight corners and sheer drops were not for the faint of heart. But now that the highway has been widened and somewhat straightened, few are daunted, and many make the drive just to gaze at the views across the Gulf Islands towards the mainland. This area, too, seemed perfect for a country inn: The Aerie, Mediterranean in style, west-coast in execution, perches above the road, looking across magnificent forest, hills and water.

Neither James Douglas nor those weary miners would have accorded Long Beach the accolades they heaped on Victoria. Imbued with the Biblical idea of Eden as a bucolic garden where flowers bloomed and fruit rained from the trees, they were dismayed by the depth and drama of the rainforest and fearful of the surging seas and rocky coastline that too often threatened their ships. Nor did the west coast welcome would-be gardeners: as decades passed, the few hardy settlers of European origin who tried to convert forest clearings into cultivated spaces

above: Artwork in Market Square, a revitalized heritage space in downtown Victoria.

almost all gave up in disgust and retreated to more hospitable surroundings.

But if Eden is not just a garden, but also a place of great plenty, then the west coast too deserves this title. The First Nations people who have lived here for thousands of years certainly saw things this way. Whales, seals and sea lions; salmon, halibut and rockfish; crabs, mussels and clams; berries, ferns and roots; cedar bark for weaving and cedar logs for building houses and canoes and creating art: everything they needed, this paradise offered them.

It took a little longer for non-natives to appreciate the lure of Vancouver Island's west coast. Much of that coast is still inaccessible by road. Deep inlets that slash inland make it almost impossible to build a road that parallels the Pacific. North of Port Renfrew, at the end of the Sooke road from Victoria, only one  such road exists, the forty-two kilometres that stretch along the outer edge of the anvil-shaped land between the towns of Ucluelet and Tofino. For decades, residents of these towns lived from logging and fishing. No road joined their beaches and coves to the island's east coast until 1959; that first road was dirt, winding, muffler-breaking, with drop-offs that gave pause to many a would-be explorer.

Then, in 1971, much of the coast between the two small towns became part of Pacific Rim National Park, some 50,000 hectares set aside to preserve the Pacific landscape of ocean, islands and rainforest. When the road west from Port Alberni was improved and paved in 1972, visitors flocked to discover the magnificent cedars and Sitka spruce, the long sandy beaches, and the waves that pounded onto rocky headlands. Now more than half a million people cross the island every year to visit the Long Beach sector of the park.

Clearly, the few motels, hotels and campgrounds in the area could not accommodate the crowds. New accommodations, including a flood of small inns and bed-and-breakfasts, along with restaurants, art galleries and tour 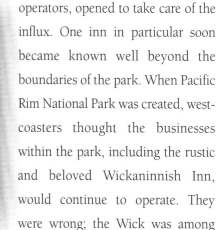 operators, opened to take care of the influx. One inn in particular soon became known well beyond the boundaries of the park. When Pacific Rim National Park was created, west-coasters thought the businesses within the park, including the rustic and beloved Wickaninnish Inn, would continue to operate. They were wrong; the Wick was among those forced to close. The McDiarmid family, headed by Tofino doctor Howard McDiarmid, who also served as a member of the provincial legislature, vowed to build a new Wickaninnish. That inn, just south of Tofino, opened in 1996.

Though James Douglas and the nineteenth-century miners might not recognize as paradise a place where whales breech offshore and trees rise to a hundred metres in height, those who visit this region now are rapidly discovering another definition of Eden, one that encompasses wild beauty and natural plenty.

above: The leaves and roots of false lily-of-the-valley, a denizen of Sitka spruce forests and shady woods, were used by native peoples to make medicines and potions.

following page: The domes and turrets of Victoria's Parliament Buildings look out over the building lawn, the harbour and downtown Victoria.

above: A sailboat tests the wind and waves
in Victoria's annual Swiftsure International
Yacht Race.
opposite page: Victoria by night.

following page: The Vancouver Island
mountains at dusk.

below: A horse-drawn carriage takes tourists
around the downtown.

The Mediterranean touch:
THE AERIE

The land falls sharply east from the rocky and forested heights of the Malahat Ridge to the deep turquoise waters of fjord-like Finlayson Arm, on the southeast coast of Vancouver Island. The view is distinctively Pacific coast–but, for Maria Schuster, it prompted memories of another scene, north of Milan, where Alpine slopes plunge to Lake Lugano. That resemblance, glimpsed on a chance visit, led to the creation of The Aerie, a Mediterranean-styled country inn on Vancouver Island.

In 1984, Maria was running a resort in the Bahamas and looking for a new location, one where she and her former husband Leo could eventually retire. They made an ideal team to create and run an inn. She came from hotel management in Europe, where at age twenty-six she had been the youngest ever female manager of a five-star property; he had been classically trained in some of the finest kitchens in Europe, and held executive chef positions in Sweden, France, Portugal, Egypt, Canada and the Bahamas.

Friends suggested they might look at the Pacific Northwest; Maria and Leo visited Vancouver Island. Their trips along the spectacular Malahat Drive converted them: they returned several times, seeking the perfect property. That they found it between Finlayson

Arm and Shawnigan Lake confounded the locals, who could not imagine a luxurious resort succeeding in a region more noted for lakeside cabins.

High on a forested hillside, they built a Mediterranean-styled villa; a few years later, the resort expanded. Now, The Aerie is a nineteen-suite, ten-room inn with a famed restaurant, a succession of white buildings with tiled roofs contoured into a terraced slope, oriented so that restaurant, rooms, terraces, gazebos, even the swimming pool, all look out over the fabled view of hills, water and distant mountains. A member of the prestigious Relais & Châteaux association of small inns and resorts, The Aerie regularly appears in lists of best places to stay, best places to dine.

Beside one of the terraced reflecting pools stands a slim sleek heron, sculpted of wood. The artist is of Norwegian origin, adopted as a child into a Cowichan First Nations family. That combination captures the harmony of borrowing from Europe, staying attuned to the land. The Schusters did not want to imitate the great Canadian lodges, with their log-cabin styles. Instead they chose to integrate classic continental design with west–coast themes. The suites may contain oversized down sofas, leather sleigh beds with Christian Dior down duvets or Persian carpets, but the

opposite page: The private dining room at
The Aerie.

above: The Mediterranean-style villas of
The Aerie are contoured into the hillside.

above: The Aerie looks out over Finlayson
Arm, the Gulf Islands and the mainland
mountains beyond.

slate carvings at the doors are of Vancouver Island rock, and wood from island trees is incorporated into each building. Outside, the garden design reminds of Mediterranean rock gardens, but many of the plants are native to the northwest.

A hiking trail climbs through thirty forested hectares to a viewpoint across the Saanich Peninsula, Victoria, the Olympic Mountains, Mount Baker and Mount Rainier–a sweeping panorama of the forests, straits and mountains of the Pacific Northwest.

A European interpretation of a Pacific coast theme also inspires the cuisine, served in a series of small dining rooms. Maria's son Markus Griesser, who manages The Aerie, and his chefs use the best of local ingredients, buying from about sixty farms: lamb, veal, venison, ostrich, emu, game birds, rabbit, vegetables. Fish and shellfish come from the ocean; mushrooms, fiddleheads and berries from the forests. A long and superb wine list features wines from Vancouver Island, other British Columbia vineyards, the Pacific coast, and around the world.

Griesser is passionate about the farmers he has found, noting with pride that they can supply such exotics as thirty varieties of lettuce and fifty types of heritage apples. He is particularly inspired by the Cowichan Valley just to the north, a sunny valley which has, he thinks, the potential to become a little Provence, and has teamed with valley farmers to create farm and vineyard tours.

His passion and belief in the region match his mother's sense of discovery those many years ago, when she first espied the view from the Malahat and determined to create an inn that has become known around the world.

above: The continental elegance of The Aerie's small dining rooms.

above: Boats anchored off Sidney Spit, where
their occupants can enjoy sun and warm waters.

opposite page: Snow-covered Red Pillar Rock
soars from Vancouver Island's mountainous spine.

following page: A fish boat heads back to shore
after a day's work.

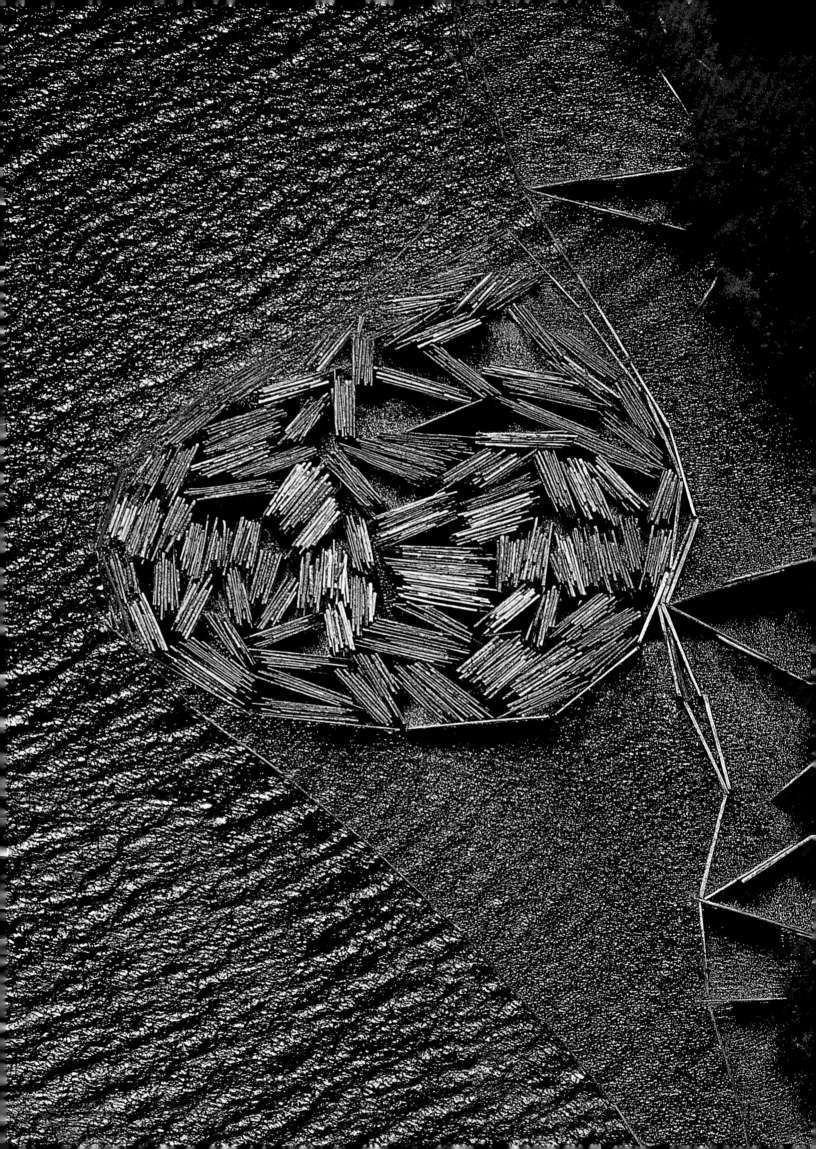

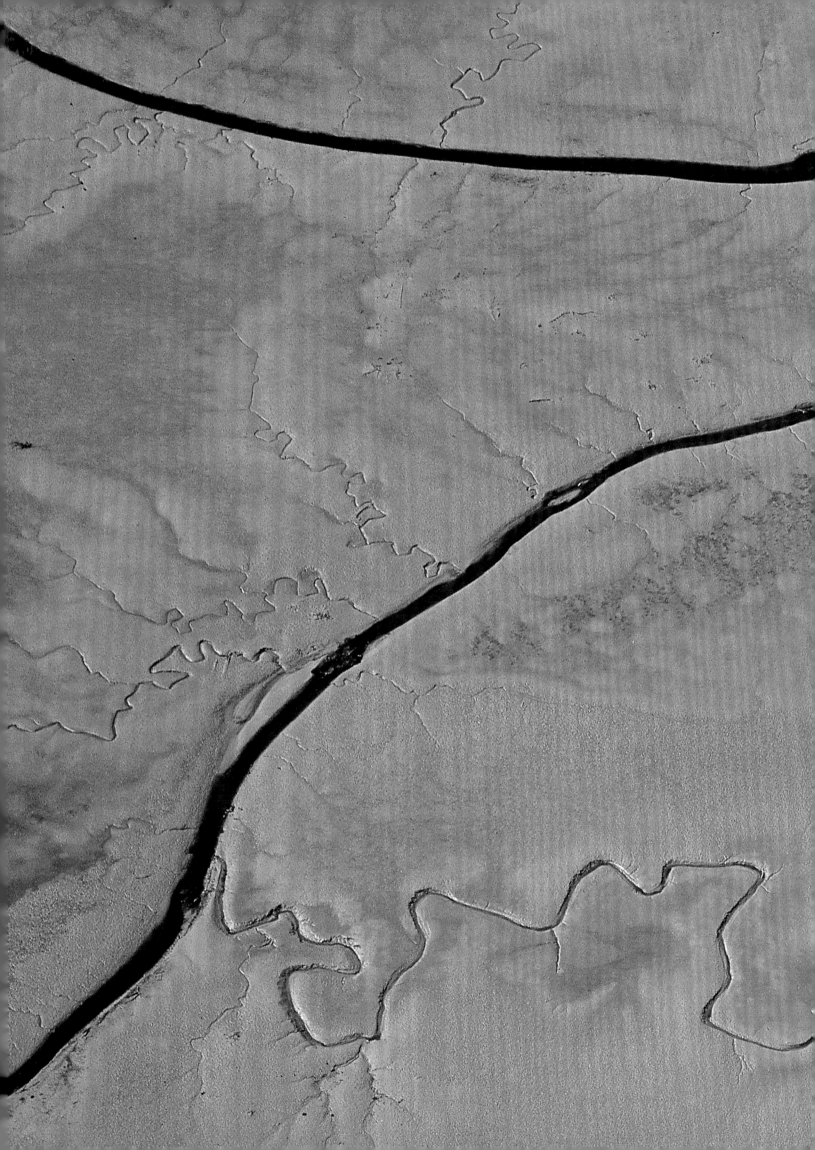

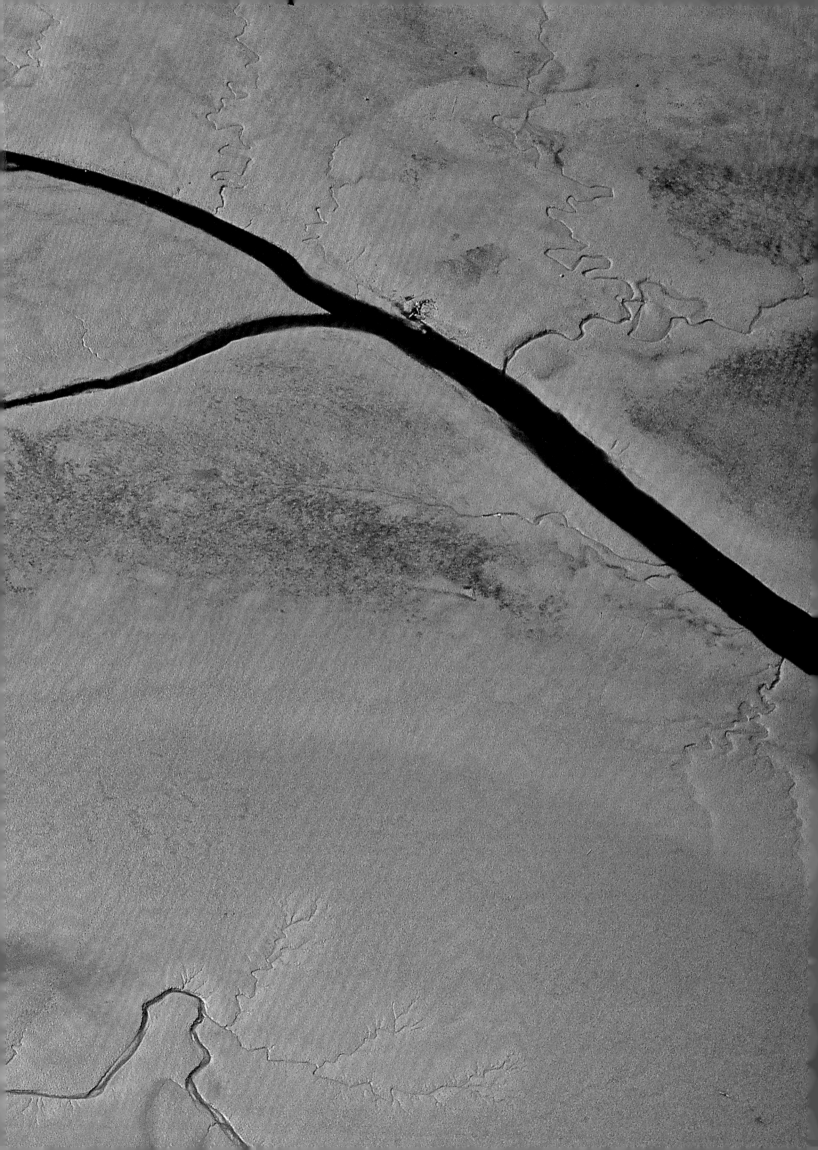

above: Barnacles have found a home on this silvered shell.

previous page: Patterns on the muddy tidal flats
near Tofino.